Top Tips for Weaning

Top Tips for Weaning

Gina Ford

Vermilion
LONDON

3 5 7 9 10 8 6 4 2

Published in 2011 by Vermilion, an imprint of Ebury Publishing

Ebury Publishing is a Random House Group company

Copyright © Gina Ford 2011

Gina Ford has asserted her right to be identified as the author of this work in accordance with the Copyright, Designs and Patents Act 1988.

The Random House Group Limited Reg. No. 954009

Addresses for companies within the Random House Group can be found at www.rbooks.co.uk

A CIP catalogue record for this book is available from the British Library

The Random House Group Limited supports The Forest Stewardship
Council (FSC), the leading international forest certification organisation. All our
titles that are printed on Greenpeace-approved FSC certified paper carry the FSC logo.
Our paper procurement policy can be found at www.rbooks.co.uk/environment

Mixed Sources
Product group from well-managed
forests and other controlled sources
www.fsc.org Cert no. TT-COC-2139
© 1996 Forest Stewardship Council

Printed and bound in Great Britain by CPI Mackays, Chatham, ME5 8TD

ISBN 9780091935139

To buy books by your favourite authors and register for offers, visit www.rbooks.co.uk

Contents

Acknowledgements

I would like to express my thanks and gratitude to the thousands of parents whom I have worked with or advised over the years. Their constant feedback, opinions and suggestions have been an enormous help in writing my books.

I would also like to thank my publisher Fiona MacIntyre and editor Louise Coe for their constant encouragement and faith in my work, and thanks to the rest of the team at Vermilion for all their hard work on the book.

Special thanks are also owed to my agent Emma Kirby, for her dedication and support, and to Laura Simmons, for her efforts in gathering information for the book. Thank you to Kate Brian, the website editor of Contentedbaby.com, Jane Waygood and Rory Jenkins, and the rest of the team at Contentedbaby.com, for their support while I was writing this book and their wonderful work on the website.

And, finally, I am ever grateful for the huge support I receive from the thousands of readers of my books who take the time to contact me – a huge thank you to you all and much love to your contented babies.

Introduction

To establish long-term healthy eating habits for your baby you will need to put a lot of thought into the early stages of weaning – not only into the types of food you introduce, but also at which age they are introduced.

In my experience a great many feeding difficulties stem from the lack of structure of milk feeding in the early days, leading to parents introducing solids too early and decreasing their baby's milk intake too rapidly, thereby depriving him of the vital nutrients offered by milk. Another common problem is babies being introduced to solids too late. This results in the baby drinking vast amounts of milk and refusing solids long past a time when it is essential he is taking them.

The Department of Health in the UK now advises that babies should be exclusively breast-fed for the first six months of life. Between six and nine months, it is recommended that babies are introduced to a variety of different foods, gradually reducing the amount of milk they take until they become established on three meals a day.

By one year, the theory is that a baby should be eating much the same food as the rest of the family. Sadly, however, for a large number of parents this is not the case and a great many find that by the time their baby reaches toddlerhood mealtimes have become a battlefield involving much cajoling, tears and tantrums as worried parents try to persuade their children to eat small amounts of healthy foods. Evidence of this can be seen regularly on our screens via the many parenting programmes that highlight these problems, or in newspapers and magazines which report that our children's diet is worse now than it was in the 1950s – and a large number of teenagers are facing many serious health issues as a result of unhealthy eating habits in early life.

The feedback I have had over the years via my consultancy service and website www.contentedbaby.com is that the

Contented Little Baby (CLB) weaning plan has worked for thousands of babies around the globe. In this top tips book I have devised a new plan that fits in with the current recommendations to wean at six months. I realise, however, that all babies are individuals and in certain circumstances some parents are advised by their health visitor or GP to wean earlier than this. To ensure that milk remains the most important source of food for your baby, I have included clear guidance on which are the best foods to introduce and at what time, so that your baby's milk intake is not reduced too rapidly.

The book takes you through the different stages of weaning, showing you what to do at each one. It also provides you with feeding plans for your baby and will help you avoid some of the common problems that many parents face during the first year. The CLB feeding plans have worked for thousands of parents, resulting in a contented baby who eats a healthy, varied diet – they can work for your baby too.

1
When to Wean

Over the last few years, the changing and often conflicting advice on when to wean a baby has caused confusion for many new parents. All parents want to establish long-term healthy eating habits for their children, and the aim of this book is to eliminate the confusion and simplify the weaning process. Weaning should and can be an enjoyable and exciting time for both baby and parents. The Contented Little Baby (CLB) methods of weaning have been successful for hundreds of thousands of parents around the world. Following the advice and the tried-and-tested top tips in this book should take the worry out of weaning, and will result in a happy, contented baby who enjoys a healthy and wide-ranging diet.

The most recent Department of Health (DoH) guidelines recommend exclusive breast-feeding for the first six months (26 weeks) of a baby's life, i.e. no solids or infant formula during that time. The previous DoH advice was to wean a baby between four and six months and not to give solids before four months (17 weeks).

From the huge amount of feedback I receive from parents, it is evident that there is some confusion surrounding the latest government recommendations. Certainly, there are health professionals who believe that it is not weaning between four and six months that threatens a baby's health, but the kind of food the baby is given. It is also clear that there are some babies who do not seem to be satisfied on milk alone for the full six months, resulting in the parents struggling to cope with a miserable, fretful baby as they try to push him to six months on milk alone.

Solid food should never be given before four months (17 weeks) for the following reasons:

* It takes up to four months for the lining of a baby's gut to develop and the kidneys to mature. Introducing solids too early puts pressure on these organs.

* Experts believe that introducing solids too early can put a baby at a higher risk of developing allergies.

* Before weaning, your baby needs to have good head and neck control and should be able to sit upright, supported, in a chair to reduce the risk of choking. This is rare in babies under four months.

* Scientists in Scotland found that a persistent cough was more common in babies who had been given solids before 12 weeks.

* Introducing solids too soon can lead to babies cutting back too quickly on milk feeds, which should still be the main source of nutrition until six months.

* Early weaning can lead to overfeeding which, research suggests, could put your child at a higher risk of becoming obese in later life and increase his risk of getting cancer, diabetes, heart disease, etc.

If your baby is six months old (or between four and six months, under guidance from your health visitor or GP) he may be ready for weaning if:

* He has doubled his birth weight and weighs over 6.8kg (15lb), and your health visitor is happy with his weight gain each week.

* He has been taking a full feed from both breasts, or a 240ml (8oz) formula feed, four or five times a day, but still appears to be hungry.

* He has been sleeping well at night and at nap times but is waking up earlier and earlier.

If you and your health visitor agree that you should not introduce solids until six months, it is important to satisfy your baby's increased hunger by introducing further milk feeds. Increase the 10/10.30pm feed if you have not already done so. Babies who are taking a full feed at 10/10.30pm and waking in the middle of the night may need a further milk feed in the early hours to get them through to 7am.

In order to meet your baby's increased hunger in the daytime, you should feed him at 6/7am, then bring his next feed forward to 10am and offer him a top-up feed prior to his lunchtime nap. He should then be offered another feed at 2/2.30pm, and then, instead of a full feed after the bath, offered a split feed at 5/6.15pm. Introducing these two split feeds in the morning and evening will increase his overall daily milk intake and help satisfy his hunger.

It is more difficult to tell how much milk a baby who is being breast-fed exclusively is receiving. If your baby is over four months and showing most of the above signs that he is ready for weaning, you will need to talk to your health visitor or GP about the choices available to you.

Early weaning

If you have been advised to wean early, it is important to remember that milk is still the most important food for your baby as it provides the right balance of vitamins and minerals. Solids given before six months should be classed as 'first tastes and fillers' in addition to full milk feeds.

Always offer a full milk feed first, before solids, to ensure that your baby's daily milk intake does not decrease too rapidly. A baby being weaned early will still need a milk feed at 10/10.30pm until solids are well established. Babies who are weaned between four and six months are usually able to drop the late feed earlier than babies who start solids at six months.

Introducing solids

* Introduce solids after the 10/11am milk feed so that your baby has had nearly half of his daily intake of milk before noon, thus ensuring that he doesn't cut back his milk intake too quickly.

* To avoid problems with your baby's digestion, and so that you can identify any allergic reactions, introduce only one new food every three days.

* Studies have shown that a high-fruit diet can lead to diarrhoea and slow growth in babies, so keep the solids weighted towards baby rice and puréed vegetables. Too much fruit can also lead to a sweet tooth.

* All baby food must be salt free, and sugar only used in small quantities for stewing very sour fruit. If you are using ready-made baby foods, these are required by law to be salt-free. However, do check the labels, as some are bulked out with unnecessary fillers, such as starch and fruit juices.

* Meat, chicken or fish should not be introduced until your baby is capable of digesting reasonable amounts of other solids, and usually not until after six months of age. If you start to wean at the recommended age of six months, you will need to work through the first stage foods much quicker, so that your baby is used to digesting a reasonable amount of vegetables, cereals and fruit before protein is introduced. When your baby is having around six tablespoons of mixed vegetables at 'lunch', protein can be introduced.

* Dairy products, eggs, wheat, nuts and citrus fruits should not be given until after six months of age as they are likely to trigger allergies. If you have a history of allergies in your family, discuss when to introduce these foods with your health visitor.

* Symptoms of allergies include rashes, wheezing, coughing, runny nose, sore bottom, diarrhoea, irritability and swelling of the eyes. However, these symptoms can also be caused by house-mites, animal fur, wool and certain soaps and

household cleaning products, so don't leap to any conclusions – consult your GP.

* Honey should never be given to a baby under 12 months because of the risk of infant botulism.

* Increase amounts of solid food gradually (see page 37).

* Babies who are weaned before six months should have their solids increased by no more than two or three teaspoonfuls a week to ensure that their milk does not decrease too quickly. Babies weaned at six months can have their solids increased at a much faster rate. As a general guideline, most babies should be taking 6–8 tablespoons of solids between the ages of six and seven months, when protein is introduced.

* Avoid regular use of commercially prepared baby foods. They are not as energy-dense as home-cooked meals, nor do they provide your baby with experience of the distinct flavours and different textures of home-made food. Many also contain large amounts of water and are likely to be

bulked out with fillers, such as rice, potato and maltodextrin (a potato starch used in the gum on postage stamps!).

Preparing and cooking food for your baby

Making your own food not only works out cheaper but, more importantly, will be of greater nutritional benefit to your baby. Also, if you make up large quantities at a time and store mini-meals away in the freezer, preparing food for your baby needn't be fiddly or time-consuming.

The following list of equipment will help make preparing your baby's first foods easier:

❀ Sterilising solution – for sterilising pans, ice-cube trays and freezer containers.

❀ Ice-cube trays – buy trays that allow for 15ml (1 tablespoon) in each 'cube' as I refer to these amounts in the weaning guidelines for each stage.

- A tablespoon measure – a 15ml spoon – takes the guess-work out of serving sizes.

- Freezer-proof containers.

- A hand-held blender – great for puréeing or pulsing meals in the pan before measuring out and freezing. Get one with a good motor and a detachable chopping blade so that it can be easily sterilised.

Sterilising feeding equipment

All feeding equipment should be sterilised for the first six months, and bottles and teats for as long as they are used. This can be done by either:

- boiling items in a large pan of water for five minutes,

- soaking utensils in sterilising solution for 30 minutes (or according to the manufacturer's instructions), or

- using a steam steriliser.

After six months, the recommendation is to wash all items in a dishwasher, or rinse hand-washed items with boiling water from the kettle.

Packing food for the freezer

* Make sure that cooked, puréed food is covered as quickly as possible and transfer it to the freezer as soon as it is cool enough.

* Never put warm food into a refrigerator or freezer.

* Your freezer should be at a temperature of -18°C.

* If using an ice-cube tray, fill it with puréed food, open-freeze until solid, and then pop the cubes out of the tray into a sterilised freezer container. Non-sterilised items, such as plastic freezer bags, can be used from six months. Seal well and freeze.

* Label items clearly with the date they were prepared and a 'use by' date of six weeks later.

* Never refreeze cooked food. Food can only be put back into the freezer if it was originally frozen raw, then defrosted and cooked – a raw frozen chicken breast, defrosted, for example, can be frozen as a cooked casserole.

Defrosting tips

* Ideally, defrost frozen food in the fridge overnight.

* If you have forgotten to take it out of the freezer, leave it at room temperature and transfer it to the fridge as soon as it has defrosted.

* Make sure food is covered at all times and stand it on a plate to catch any drips.

* Never be tempted to speed up the defrosting process by putting food into warm or hot water.

* Always use defrosted food within 24 hours.

Reheating tips

* When batch cooking, take out a portion of food for your baby to use now and freeze the rest.

* Never be tempted to reheat leftovers.

* Foods should only be re-heated once.

Please remember, babies are much more susceptible than adults to food poisoning, so get into the habit of throwing leftovers or unused food away immediately.

Weaning guidelines

The following guidelines will help you establish the right foods at the right age for your baby. Once you have read the guidelines, you can then use them alongside the weaning plan that is appropriate for your baby's age.

* Introduce solids after the 11am feed. Prepare everything you need in advance: baby chair, two bibs, two spoons and a clean, damp cloth.

* Start by offering your baby one teaspoonful of pure organic baby rice mixed to a very smooth consistency using either expressed milk, formula milk or cooled boiled water. The baby is more likely to take to it if it has the familiar taste of milk.

* Make sure the baby rice is cool enough before feeding it to your baby. Use a shallow plastic spoon – never a metal one, which can be too sharp or get too hot.

* Some babies need help in learning how to feed from the spoon. Place the spoon just far enough into your baby's mouth and bring it up and out against the roof of his mouth; his upper gums will take the food off, and this will encourage him to feed.

* Once your baby is established on baby rice at 11am, give the rice after the 6pm feed instead. When giving solids

at 6pm, give the baby most of his milk first, and then offer solids.

✿ Once he is taking two teaspoonfuls of baby rice mixed with milk or water after the 6pm feed, a small amount of pear purée can be introduced after the 11am feed.

✿ Assuming the pear purée is tolerated, transfer it to the 6pm feed. Mixing the purée with the baby rice in the evening will make it more palatable and prevent your baby from becoming constipated.

✿ Small amounts of various organic vegetables and fruits can now be introduced after the 11am feed. To prevent your baby developing a sweet tooth, try to give more vegetables than fruit. At this stage, avoid stronger-tasting vegetables such as broccoli or spinach. Concentrate on root vegetables such as sweet potatoes and swede as these contain natural sugars: they will taste sweeter and blander and may prove more palatable to your baby.

✿ Always be very positive and smile when offering new foods. If your baby spits a food out, it may not mean that he dislikes it. Remember this is all very new to him, and different foods will get different reactions. If he positively refuses a new food, however, leave it and try it again in a week.

2
First Stage of Weaning (Four to Six/ Seven Months)

All babies differ and have their own likes and dislikes, so don't feel anxious if your child doesn't fit in exactly with the plan. If your baby refuses a particular food, leave it for a week or so, then try again.

The following are all ideal 'first taste' solids (i.e. from four months if advised to wean early):

* pure organic baby rice

* pear

* apple

* carrot

* sweet potato

* potatoes

* green beans

* courgettes

* swede

Once your baby is happily tolerating these foods, you can introduce the following (i.e. from five months if advised to wean early):

* oats

* parsnips

* mango

* peaches

- broccoli
- avocado
- barley
- peas
- cauliflower

If you are weaning early, always offer milk first at both the 11am and 6pm feeds, as this is still the most important food, in nutritional terms, at this stage. While appetites do vary, the majority of babies will be drinking 840–900ml (28–30oz) of formula a day, or four or five full breast-feeds.

Babies who started weaning at the age of four months (on medical advice) should have tasted baby rice, plus a variety of vegetables and fruit, by the time they are five months. Most will, by five months, be happy to take a combination of two or three different vegetables at lunchtime.

If your baby is being weaned at four months old, you should introduce new foods every three to four days or so, increasing the amounts very gradually so that he continues to take full milk feeds.

If you started weaning at five months, work through the list of foods slightly faster, introducing a new food every three days. You should then move on to the foods suitable for a five-month-old once your baby has had all the foods suitable from four months.

If you started weaning at six months, you will need to work through the listed foods much more quickly, introducing a new food every two days, and increasing the amounts rapidly.

If you are weaning at six months, you should go straight into the tier method of feeding at the 11am feed. This is when you offer the baby half his milk first, then give him most of his solids. For the remainder of the meal, alternate between his milk and solids until it is all gone (or until he turns his head away indicating that he is full up). Continue to offer most of his milk first at the 6pm feed.

Introducing solids in the evening

Within a couple of days of introducing baby rice at 11am (or after three or four days if advised to wean early), you should progress to offering solids in the evening as well. Offer 1–2 teaspoons of baby rice initially and then mix this with a cube of fruit purée as the first week progresses.

Giving solids after your baby has taken most of his 6pm (bedtime) feed will encourage him to cut back on his 10pm feed, which will have a knock-on effect of him being hungrier for his first milk feed of the day.

Every second day, increase the amount of rice your baby is having at bedtime. On alternate days, increase his lunchtime solids. Remember that the baby rice is far more filling than fruit, so increase that more rapidly than the fruit.

As your baby increases the amount of solids he is taking at this time, you should automatically see a decrease in the amount of milk he takes at the 10pm feed. If he does not cut back of his own accord, I suggest that you reduce his 10pm feed gradually by 15ml (½oz) every couple of nights provided, of course, that he continues to sleep through to 7am.

Gradually, over a couple of weeks (or after your baby reaches six months if you weaned early), move the solids back to 5.30pm, with half the milk before the solids and the other half of the milk after his bath.

By seven months (or earlier if you were advised to wean early), you will be working towards replacing the fruit and rice with a proper tea at 5pm. At this point your baby will be having a drink of cooled boiled water or well-diluted pure fruit juice from a beaker, instead of milk, at this time.

Weaning at six to seven months

Starting weaning at six months coincides with the age that a baby's natural store of iron, with which he is born, is getting very low. Therefore, if you follow current guidelines and wait until your baby is six months before commencing weaning, it is important to progress through the first stage weaning foods quickly to ensure that your baby is introduced to iron-rich foods by the time he is seven months old.

Within a couple of days of introducing baby rice, you should progress quickly through the food groups, introducing a new food every couple of days and increasing the amounts he is having at the same rate.

The tier system of feeding at lunchtime (see page 38) will encourage your baby to increase his solids more rapidly. If you do not reduce your baby's milk intake at this feed, you may find that he becomes very fussy about weaning and rejects many of the foods you are introducing.

Continue to decrease the amount of milk he is taking at the 11am feed, until he is happy to start with his solids at lunchtime. Once he is taking four to six cubes he should have cut the amount of milk he is taking after the solids, until he is only having a few minutes on the breast or a couple of ounces of formula.

If your baby is fussy about solids but still taking four or five milk feeds a day, it is important to reduce the amount of milk he is taking as this will improve his appetite for the solids.

You should only offer him half his milk at 11am to encourage his interest in solid food at this time.

You should aim to have your baby on two meals a day within a couple of weeks of starting solids. By the time he reaches seven months, regardless of when he began weaning, all babies should be well established on two meals a day, progressing to three meals consisting of a wide variety of foods from the different food groups. You should also aim to have reduced your baby's milk intake to three milk feeds a day (breakfast, mid-afternoon and bedtime).

The 10pm feed

Many babies continue to need a feed at 10pm to get them through the night until solids are well established. If your baby is following the Contented Little Baby (CLB) routines during the day and sleeping through from 7pm to 7am with only a small feed at 10/10.30pm, then introducing solids and weaning him off this late feed should be fairly simple.

As the amount of solids he takes at teatime increases, the amount of milk he wants at the late feed should decrease. If he does not cut back automatically, as long as he is sleeping through to 7am, you can gradually reduce the amount he is taking. For breast-fed babies, reduce the feed by a few minutes, and for formula-fed babies you should reduce the amount offered by 30ml (1oz). Provided he sleeps through, you can continue to reduce this feed by this amount every three nights.

Once you reach a stage where your baby has slept through for several nights on a very short breast-feed (five minutes) or a formula-feed of a couple of ounces, you should be able to cut the feed out altogether without worrying about him waking up hungry before 7am.

With babies who are taking a full feed, it may take at least three to four weeks to eliminate it. There is no benefit in reducing it too quickly and having your baby waking up earlier.

If your baby is not cutting down on his 10pm feed once solids are introduced, it may be that he is not getting the right quantities of solids for his age and weight, or too small a feed at 6.30pm. Keep a diary of all food and milk consumed over a period of four days to help pinpoint why he is not dropping that last feed.

If your baby is taking a full feed at 10pm – with the knock–on effect of only taking a small milk feed at breakfast time, demanding a big milk feed at 10/11am, refusing lunchtime solids and then needing a further big milk feed at 2.30pm – it can be tempting to cut out the 10pm feed altogether, but this often results in a baby waking up hungry in the night, throwing the whole day out. It is better to drastically cut down the milk he has at 11am and 2.30pm. This will encourage him to eat more solids after the 11am milk feed, and make him more likely to want solids in the evening.

Once he is increasing the amounts of solids at mealtimes, you can gradually start to reduce the amount of milk he is taking at 10pm, using the method described above, without worrying about the risk of him waking early, genuinely hungry.

First stage tips

* During this stage, babies should taste cereal, plus a variety of fruit and vegetables.

* If weaning at six months, food still needs to be puréed but, between six and seven months, not so smoothly. This will prepare your baby for mashed food during the second stage.

* A baby may be ready to start having breakfast, once he shows signs of hunger long before his 11am feed. Organic oatmeal cereal with a small amount of puréed fruit seems to be a favourite with most babies.

* You should still give your baby most of his 7am milk feed first, even after breakfast has been introduced.

* If your baby reaches seven months and shows no signs of wanting breakfast, it would be wise to reduce his 6/7am milk feed very slightly and offer a small amount of solids.

* Your baby still needs a minimum of 600ml (20oz) of milk a day. Throughout the first stage, give milk feeds at breakfast,

lunch, mid-afternoon and evening, supplementing with vegetable purée at lunch and baby rice and fruit purée in the evening.

> **Case Study: Polly, aged six months**
> **Problem: Low milk intake**
> **Cause: Introducing formula milk and solids too quickly, which leads to a reduction in the mother's milk supply**
>
> *Polly weighed just over 3.6kg (8lb) at birth; she took to the breast well and regained her birth weight within eight days. She was a very placid, easy baby and fell naturally into a routine of her own accord. By the time she was three weeks old she was settling well at 6.30pm, waking around midnight, feeding well and settling back to sleep until 5.30am. This continued until Polly was*

nearly six weeks old, when she suddenly started to wake up around 10pm demanding a feed. She would then wake up again around 2am and 5am and refuse to settle back to sleep without a feed. This pattern continued for a further two weeks. Caroline, her mother, was becoming so exhausted getting up twice at night that she decided to follow the advice of friends and introduce a bottle of formula at the 10pm feed to see if it would get Polly back to sleeping longer in the night.

Within a week Polly had started to sleep through to 3am, and by the time she was 12 weeks she was sleeping through to 7am from her last formula feed at 10pm. By 16 weeks Polly was still sleeping through the night from the 10pm feed, but started demanding to be fed much sooner than usual during the day. With a good weight gain of 210–240g (7–8oz) each week, she was now weighing well over 6.6kg (15lb). Polly was such a good weight and was showing all the typical signs of needing to be weaned that Caroline introduced her to a small amount of baby rice and fruit at four months.

Polly loved the solids and within a week she was having solids twice a day and sleeping through to 6.30am with only a 90ml (3oz) formula feed at 10pm. Caroline decided to drop this feed, as she was sure that Polly could get through the night without it. But, as she was planning to return to work when Polly was six months, Caroline decided to introduce a bottle of formula at the 2pm feed, so Polly continued to take some of her milk from a bottle. She was very reluctant to take this bottle and would never drink more than 90ml (3oz) at this feed. However, her weight gain was still good and she continued to sleep from 7pm to 6.30am, so Caroline was not overly concerned about this.

At six months, when Caroline returned to work, she

introduced protein at Polly's 11am feed and replaced the breast-feed with a drink of cooled boiled water. Polly was now having a breast-feed at 6.30am and 6.30pm, and a bottle of formula at 2.30pm. Within a week of commencing the new feeding pattern, Polly began waking up at 5am. Caroline attempted to settle her back to sleep by patting her or offering her water, but this rarely worked. Such an early start to the day resulted in Polly being very grumpy and overtired by the time Caroline got home from work at 4pm, and wanting to go to sleep at 6pm in the evening.

When I received Polly's feeding chart it was obvious that the reason for her 5am waking was one of genuine hunger caused by the sudden drop in her daily milk intake. I believed that there were two reasons for the reduction in her milk intake. The first was that, unlike most babies, Polly did not automatically increase the amount she drank at the 2.30pm feed when the 11.30am feed was dropped. The second reason was that her mother's milk supply had decreased very rapidly when she started work and went down to two breast-feeds a day. This meant that in addition to the too-small feed at 2.30pm, Polly was not getting enough milk at the 6.30pm feed, resulting in a genuine need to feed at 5am.

Unfortunately, because solid food had been introduced at the same time as the formula feed at 2.30pm, the combination filled Polly up so much that it made her less keen to take milk from a bottle at this feed. Introducing a second lot of solids at 5pm, within a week of introducing the first lot of solids, meant that she very quickly cut down on the amount of milk she took from the breast at 6pm, resulting in a 5am waking through a genuine need for a milk feed. Although Caroline's breasts were very full in the morning and Polly did take *a good feed at this time, she could not take enough in this one feed to compensate for the big drop at her other two feeds. By the time Polly reached six months she was having three solid meals a day.*

A baby of six months still needs at least three full milk feeds a day, and some may need up to five if they have not been weaned. Milk is still very important at this stage and it is vital that it is not replaced too quickly with solids, which is what happened in Polly's case. The problem was made worse by the fact that she was introduced to formula at the same time as she was quickly put on two solid meals a day. This also affected the amount of breast milk that Caroline was producing. Replacing the 2.30pm feed with formula and introducing solids twice a day within such a short time meant that Polly very quickly started to take less and less from the breast, resulting in Caroline's milk supply decreasing very rapidly. She was very keen to breast-feed Polly in the morning and the evening until she was a year old, but was anxious that this was not going to be possible if her milk production kept decreasing as Polly increased her solids.

I explained to Caroline that the first thing we had to do was to boost her milk supply so that Polly did not continue to increase her intake of solids too quickly. Since Caroline was at work from 10am to 4pm, it was not possible to put Polly to the breast more frequently during the day, and expressing at work was not an option. I suggested that she should express in the evening before bedtime and use that milk for Polly's 2.30pm feed in the afternoon. She should then offer her both breasts at 5/5.30pm before offering solids: this would ensure that Polly did not fill up with solids, which were reducing her milk intake too much at bedtime. At 7pm she should then be offered the breast again, before being offered a top-up of formula milk. I advised Caroline to keep following this plan until Polly was taking at least 180ml (6oz) of expressed milk at the 2.30pm feed. Once she was taking this, she could then start to give Polly her solids first at 5pm, as she should have had two-thirds of her daily requirement of milk by this time.

I also advised Caroline to keep a very close watch on the amount of solids she gave Polly at 5pm as it was important that she did not increase them so quickly that the baby refused to take a good milk feed from both breasts at bedtime.

Caroline continued with this feeding pattern for a further two months, at which stage she felt that she could gradually decrease, then cut out, the 10pm expressing and reintroduce a formula feed at 2.30pm without it causing a sudden decrease in Polly's morning and evening breast-feed.

This is a very common problem for many mothers who are returning to work. I always advise those who wish to breast-feed for longer than four months to include at least one expressing during the day once their baby is weaned on to solids as this helps to maintain a good milk supply, which can otherwise decrease very rapidly once a breast-feeding mother returns to work. I also recommend not replacing a breast-feed with a formula-feed at the same time as introducing solids. I believe that the introduction of formula milk and two solid meals a day in such a short period of time severely affected Polly's appetite for her other breast-feeds, quickly reducing the amount of milk that Caroline was producing. It would have been better for Caroline to establish a full formula-feed at 2.30pm and wait until Polly went through her next growth spurt before introducing solids, as this would have allowed more time for Polly's digestive system to adjust to the formula, and more time for her to establish full feeds at the remaining two breast-feeds.

Cutting back on formula

It is quite natural for a baby to cut back on his formula intake after starting solids – it's the beginning of a process that will see him gradually increase his food intake and decrease formula/milk intake until he is eating an adult diet of solid food with little or no milk. While babies generally regulate their intake of formula to meet their needs, as a rough guide a five- to six-month-old will have four or five feeds a day of about 180–240ml (6–8oz) formula each, or four or five breast-feeds. The amount of milk your baby takes may at first fluctuate but then return to his usual level or close to it. Babies' appetites do fluctuate, and from six to seven months, as the intake of solids increases, the amount of formula required will start to fall – an appropriate level to aim for then is about 600ml (20oz).

Increase the amount of food given at meals very slowly – food given before six months of age is really more to get used to different tastes and the process of eating than to provide a large amount of nutrition. If your baby's formula intake continues to drop, you could try offering formula before food when feeding your baby, at least for the next few weeks. As another option, you could keep the food intake at the same level for a few days, rather than increasing quantities. I would suggest you do this rather than stop offering food as he has been enjoying it and will now be used to it.

If you haven't done so yet, try adding formula to baby rice and to thin down fruit and vegetable purées. It's a handy way to increase your baby's formula intake if he's not drinking as much as he should. It is always important to monitor your baby to ensure his fluid intake is sufficient, but particularly so when his intake is changing, whether due to illness, weaning or any other factor – good indicators of an adequate fluid intake are regular and well-soaked nappies, urine that is clear or straw-coloured, and a happy and alert baby.

Follow-on milk

It can be quite confusing to look at all the different formulas on shop shelves, especially as new ones appear all the time. The manufacturers of 'follow-on' formulas state that they are suitable from six months and that they contain a combination of nutrients suitable for babies of this age. Babies do start to need a slightly different nutrient mix from about six months, which neither breast milk nor a 'starter' infant formula can supply. Probably the biggest change is in iron requirements. Iron is an essential mineral for all of us, especially for its role in oxygen transport around the body. Babies are born with a good store of iron, but much of it is used up during their first six months as they get very little from their diet of breast milk or starter formulas. Thus babies require a better source of iron from about six months, and this is one of the reasons it's recommended that they start solids at this time. By introducing a range of different foods during the weaning process (following the guidelines of just one new food at a time and using suitable textures, of course) you will gradually give your little one more and more foods containing a range of nutrients, some of which will be rich in iron. Particularly good sources of iron that can be suitable for babies are iron-fortified baby rice, minced beef or lamb, oil-rich fish such as sardines, egg (be sure it's fully cooked), lentils, and green leafy vegetables such as spinach or broccoli. Do note that iron is more easily absorbed from meat than other food types. However, if iron-rich plant-based foods such as green vegetables or lentils are eaten along with a food rich in vitamin C, this will help the body to absorb the iron. Good sources of vitamin C include oranges (and their juice), berries, kiwi fruit and melon, as well as raw peppers and tomatoes. See *The*

Contented Child's Food Bible for more information on ensuring a good iron intake for your child.

So do you need to use a follow-on formula to supply extra nutrients such as iron to your baby? If he takes to solids well and, after a few months, is enjoying a range of different foods, try to ensure that he is offered a few iron-rich foods each day; this should meet his needs. Then there is no need to discontinue the formula he enjoys to change to a follow-on one. If your baby is not so keen on solids, though, or is slow to gain weight, there would be no harm in changing to a follow-on formula, as long as your baby is happy with it. They are nutritionally complete, which means that they do supply all the vitamins, minerals and protein your baby requires from formula at this stage. In this case, I'd also suggest discussing your baby's diet with your GP or health visitor, just to be on the safe side.

3
Second Stage of Weaning (Six/Seven to Nine Months)

Provided you do not have a history of allergies in your family, wheat-based cereals, pasta and bread can now be introduced to your baby's diet. Fruit need not be cooked and puréed – it can now simply be mashed – and you can introduce fresh apricots, melon, plums and dried apricots, which have been soaked overnight, as well as well-diluted unsweetened fruit juices. Try to expand the range of vegetables you are serving: include coloured bell peppers, pumpkin, cabbage and, later, spinach, Brussels sprouts, celery and (provided there is no history of allergies) tomatoes. Fish, meat and pulses can be introduced. Use mild-tasting chicken, cod or haddock (not smoked) to begin with, and then move on to lamb at seven to eight months. Red lentils, butter beans and other pulses can also be introduced at six months. Yoghurt, mild cheese and cow's milk (in cooking) can be included as well as first finger foods such as toast fingers, cooked carrot sticks, broccoli florets, pieces of soft fruit and cooked frozen mixed vegetables. Egg yolks can be introduced but must be hard-boiled.

* Small amounts of unsalted butter and/or olive oil can be introduced in cooking between six and seven months.

* You should still continue to cook all food without additional salt or sugar, although a small amount of herbs can be introduced around eight or nine months of age.

* Cow's milk should not be given as a drink until 12 months as it is too low in iron.

✿ Remember that honey should never be given to a baby under 12 months due to the risk of infant botulism.

Most babies are ready to accept stronger-tasting foods at this age. They also take pleasure from different textures, colours and presentation. Once your baby is used to taking puréed foods from a spoon, food should be mashed or 'pulsed' and kept separate to avoid mixing everything up.

When your baby is happy taking mashed food, you can start to introduce small amounts of finger food. Vegetables should be cooked until soft, then offered in cube-sized pieces or steamed and then mixed to the right consistency. As soon as your baby is managing softly cooked pieces of vegetables and soft pieces of raw fruit, you can try him with toast or a low-sugar rusk. By nine months, if your baby has several teeth, he should be able to manage some chopped raw vegetables. Dried fruit can also be given now but it must be washed first and soaked overnight.

Introducing protein

If your baby was introduced to solids before six months, by the time he reaches six months he should have tasted a wide variety of vegetables and fruit and be used to digesting reasonable amounts of carbohydrate in the form of potato and baby rice. He will be ready for the introduction of protein between six and seven months.

When your baby reaches six months (or seven months if you waited until six months to wean), you can introduce chicken, fish, meat, pulses (e.g. beans and lentils) and dairy products. Introduce these foods slowly during the early stages, trying a new food every three days to ensure that your baby does not have a bad reaction to any particular food.

Whenever possible, try to buy organic chicken and red meat, which are free from additives and growth stimulators. Pork, bacon and processed hams should not be given before 18 months as they have a high salt content.

Mixing small amounts of home-made organic chicken stock

with his vegetable purées will help prepare your baby for the different taste of protein. Start by replacing two of his lunchtime vegetable cubes (he should be having about six cubes) with two simple chicken, fish, meat or pulse recipes. Increase the amounts by one or two cubes a day until your baby's meal consists totally of one of the protein recipes.

Your baby will need one serving of animal protein a day, a serving starting at approximately 25g (1oz) and increasing to around 50g (2oz). When serving a vegetarian meal, make sure you follow the guidelines for combining vegetable protein to ensure that your baby receives a complete protein meal. It is always wise to speak to your health visitor or dietitian before giving a wholly vegetarian diet to your baby.

If you are introducing your baby to a vegetarian diet, it is important to seek expert advice on getting the balance of amino acids right. Vegetables are incomplete sources of amino acids when cooked separately, and need to be combined correctly to provide your baby with a complete source of protein.

Once you reach this stage, any milk you are still giving at this time should be replaced with a drink of water or very well-diluted pure fruit juice from a beaker (cup with a lid). Introducing a beaker at this time will prepare your baby for having all his drinks in a beaker by 12 months.

It is very easy to get into the habit of serving the same favourite foods to your baby, but this could lead to him becoming very fussy. I therefore advise that once your baby is established on the different protein meals you ensure that he receives a variety of different foods.

Second stage meals

Breakfast

As long as there is no history of allergies in your family, low sugar/salt unrefined wheat cereals can now be introduced; choose organic ones fortified with iron and B vitamins. If your baby refuses them, try adding a little mashed or grated fruit.

Alternate the cereals between oat-based and wheat-based, even if your baby shows a preference for one over the other. This avoids your baby becoming bored of having the same thing day in, day out, and also ensures variety in his diet.

You can encourage your baby to eat finger foods by offering him a little buttered toast at this stage. Once your baby is finger feeding, you can offer a selection of fruits along with lightly buttered toast fingers for breakfast.

Most babies are still desperate for their milk first thing in the morning, so still allow your baby two-thirds of his milk before breakfast. Once he is nearer nine months of age he will most likely show signs of not being hungry for milk as soon as he wakes up, and this is the time to try offering milk from a beaker, or a breast-feed, with his breakfast solids.

Lunch

If your baby is eating a proper breakfast, you will be able to push lunch to somewhere between 11.45am and 12 noon.

However, should he be eating only a small amount of breakfast, he will need to eat slightly earlier. Likewise a baby who is having only a very short nap in the morning may also need to have lunch earlier. It is important to remember that an over-tired, over-hungry baby will not feed as well, so take a cue from him as to the timing of lunch.

During this stage of weaning, you will have established protein at lunchtime. I usually find that, during the early stages of introducing protein, cooking it as a casserole with root vegetables makes it much more palatable. Many babies baulk at the strong flavour of protein which has been cooked on its own rather than mixed with vegetables.

Once protein is well established, your baby's lunchtime milk feed should be replaced with a drink of water or well-diluted juice from a beaker. You might find that he only drinks a small amount at this time, and may look for an increase of milk at the 2.30pm feed or an increase of water later in the day.

If your baby is still hungry after his main meal, offer a piece of cheese, a breadstick, chopped fruit or yoghurt.

Tea

Some babies get tired and fussy by teatime, so ensuring a well-balanced breakfast and lunch will take the strain off this meal.

At around six to seven months you will replace the fruit and rice your baby was having at 5pm with a proper tea. This meal can consist of foods such as a baked potato or pasta served with vegetables and a sauce.

Once your baby is finger feeding, tea can include a selection of mini sandwiches, breadsticks or rice cakes with a light spreading of unsalted butter, cream cheese or sugar-free jam. If he is very tired and does not eat much, try offering rice pudding or natural yoghurt with a small amount of fruit.

A small drink of water or well-diluted juice from a beaker can be offered with tea. Do not allow too large a drink at this time as it will put your baby off his last milk feed. If he starts cutting back too much on this feed, check you are not over-feeding him on solids or giving him too much to drink – his bedtime milk is still important at this stage.

Case study: Emily, aged eight months
Problem: Drinking excessive amounts of water in the night
Cause: Hunger due to over-use of commercial baby food

Emily's mother had successfully followed the Contented Little Baby routines since Emily was three weeks old and she was sleeping through the night from the 10pm feed at eight weeks. When solids were introduced at six months Emily quickly dropped the 10pm feed and slept well from 7pm to 7am. She continued to sleep and eat well until she reached seven months. She then caught a bad cold that lasted for over two weeks and resulted in lots of sleepless nights. She also started to get very fussy about her food, refusing lots of the home-cooked meals that her mother normally gave her. Desperation and concern over her poor appetite and exhaustion from weeks of sleepless nights resulted in Emily's mother giving her commercial baby food at some mealtimes. Once Emily's cold had disappeared her appetite began to improve and she very quickly developed a taste for the jars of baby food. Her mother was so pleased to see her eating normal quantities again that she started using more and more jars.

However, despite getting over her cold and eating well, Emily continued to wake up in the night, and became increasingly difficult to settle. Even when she had the cold Emily had never been fed in the night, although she had been offered cooled boiled water. Her mother was convinced that the continued wakings could not be due to hunger, but began to get very worried when Emily started drinking more and more water in the night – on some occasions she could drink as much as 180ml (6oz). On hearing her story I was not convinced that Emily's nutritional needs were being met during the day, as I had seen an increasing incidence of night-time waking in babies of her age who were being fed on jars of commercial baby food.

I explained to Emily's mother that although her daughter was taking the same quantity of commercial food as home-made food prior to her cold, the density of the food she was now having was totally different. A huge number of commercial baby meals have a high water content, and include sugar, maltodextrin and other modified starches that are used to thicken and bulk up the ingredients. The jars of chicken and lamb casserole that Emily was eating contained much less protein than the recipes her mother had been cooking for her before she caught her cold.

I convinced Emily's mother to go back to giving her home-cooked meals. However, because Emily had now developed a taste for the commercial baby food, we had to reintroduce the home-made versions very slowly. Emily's mother cooked similar recipes to her favourite jar meals, and froze them in quantities of half to one ice cube. She then very slowly introduced the home-cooked food cubes into the commercial meals, gradually increasing the amount of home-cooked food when she saw that Emily was happy taking it. It took nearly one month to get Emily totally back on to home-cooked food, but during that time her sleeping got better and she had fewer wakings in the night. By the time she was fully on a diet of home-cooked food she was back to sleeping a full 12 hours.

I have dealt with hundreds of problems similar to

Emily's. While I believe the occasional use of commercial baby food does not create problems, I am convinced that its over-use may be the cause of poor sleeping habits with some babies.

Second stage tips

* At six months your baby will have used up the store of iron he was born with, so it is important that he gets plenty of iron-rich food. To help improve iron absorption, serve cereals and meat with fruit or vegetables, and avoid giving milk at the same time as protein – it reduces the iron content by 50 per cent. If you have not weaned your baby until six months, you will need to move quickly though the food groups and introduce iron-rich food as soon as possible.

* Your baby still needs 540–600ml (18–20oz) of milk a day, inclusive of milk used in cereal and in cooking, cheese and

yoghurt. Milk feeds should be before breakfast, in the after-noon and at bedtime. Add cheese sauces, milk puddings and yoghurts if your baby is not taking enough.

* He should now be ready to sit in a high chair for meals. Always ensure he is properly strapped in and never left unattended.

* Between eight and nine months your baby may show signs of wanting to use his spoon. To encourage this, use two spoons when you feed him. Load one for your baby to try and get the food into his mouth and then use the other spoon for actually getting the food in! You can help your baby's co-ordination by holding his wrist gently and guiding the spoon into his mouth.

* By the end of nine months, a bottle-fed baby should be taking all of his breakfast milk from a beaker.

* If your baby has cut any teeth, these should be cleaned twice a day using an age-appropriate toothbrush and paste.

* Once your baby is self-feeding, it is important to wash his hands thoroughly before and after meals. He should never be left alone once he is self-feeding because of the risk of choking.

* Between seven and nine months, your baby should be eating two to three servings of carbohydrates a day. He should also have at least three servings of vegetables and fruit a day, and one serving of animal or two of vegetable protein. For information about what constitutes a serving see pages 86–7.

* A very hungry baby who is taking three full milk feeds a day plus three good solid meals may need a small drink of water and a piece of fruit mid-morning.

Using tinned fruit and vegetables

Tinned fruit and vegetables are great store-cupboard staples, always there in an emergency. Look for fruit tinned in natural juices, also vegetables tinned without added salt if possible.

And if the product does contain added salt, be sure to rinse the vegetables and discard the liquid as some salt will be dissolved in it.

Many people are concerned that tinned foods are not as nutritious as fresh ones, but this is not necessarily the case. A 1997 study by the Department of Food Science and Nutrition at the University of Illinois in the USA found that tinned fruit and vegetables were nutritionally comparable to both fresh and frozen varieties. It also looked at recipes made using tinned foods and again found that they contained similar amounts of nutrients, such as vitamins and fibre, compared to those made from fresh ingredients. While small amounts of some vitamins such as vitamin C were lost in the tinning process, once the foods were in the tins their nutrient levels were found to stay stable for at least two years.

Apart from convenience, there are other advantages to using tinned foods. The softer texture of tinned fruits such as peaches and pears can be very appealing to young children learning to eat fruit as finger foods. They also mash well as a quick baby food if you run out of fresh-cooked mashed fruit, and they blend well into smoothies. Tinned vegetables are also easy to mash or purée, and I find them invaluable for tossing into a pasta sauce or salad at the last minute when I discover that all my fresh vegetables have gone mouldy at the bottom of the refrigerator.

Eggs

Scrambled eggs make an easy and healthy meal, especially when time is short. Adding some vegetables, such as chopped tomatoes and thinly sliced courgette, along with some starchy carbohydrate food such as toast fingers, ensures that the meal is well balanced. Eggs in any form are a great source of protein and also contain valuable vitamins, including vitamin A, and minerals such as iron. Both the Government's Food Standards Agency and the British Nutrition Foundation state that eggs are suitable to introduce to children over six months of age. Of course, they should then only be given once a child is accustomed to more introductory weaning foods, such as baby rice and fruit and vegetable purées, and only in dishes with a texture that is suitable for your baby's age and weaning stage.

Eggs should not be given earlier than six months, as they are a food that people can develop allergies to. This fact can cause concern, and some people prefer to wait until their children are about eight or nine months old before giving them eggs for the first time. There's no harm in this, as long as other protein-rich foods such as meat or chicken are being eaten. Someone with a family history of allergic conditions, such as allergies, eczema or asthma, might want to delay introducing eggs until later than this and should discuss the timing with a health visitor or GP.

When serving your child eggs for the first time, you may wish to try giving the yolk and the white separately a few days apart, as they contain different types of protein. This will allow you to observe whether your child has a reaction to either part of the egg. One definite precaution to take at any child's age is to cook the eggs until hard – this is because there is a risk of salmonella, a type of food poisoning, from eggs that are not completely cooked.

4
Third Stage of Weaning (Nine to Twelve Months)

By this age your baby should be eating and enjoying all types of food, apart from those high in fat, salt and sugar. Stronger flavours, such as aubergine, beetroot, cucumber, fresh berries, garlic, pineapple, small amounts of well-diluted unsweetened orange juice and high-fibre dried fruit such as prunes and figs, can be introduced. Beef and liver can be offered but only once a week and in small amounts. You can increase the range of herbs and spices used but, again, use them in small amounts. Peanuts and honey, however, should still not be given.

It is important that your baby learns to chew properly at this stage: food should be chopped or diced, although meat still needs to be mashed, minced or very finely chopped. This is also a good time to introduce raw vegetables and salads.

Encourage your baby to learn to feed himself with finger foods and his spoon, even if the food tends to go all over the place at this stage. You should still never leave your baby alone while he is eating.

Third stage meals

Breakfast

By the time your baby reaches one year he should be taking all his drinks from a beaker with a hard spout, so try to get him used to drinking some of his breakfast milk from a beaker by the time he reaches nine months. Once he is taking all his milk from a beaker, the amount he drinks will probably go down to around 120–150ml (4–5oz), with 60–90ml (2–3oz) on his breakfast cereal.

Some babies go through a stage of refusing their breakfast cereal at this age. If this happens, try offering yoghurt and fruit instead, followed by toast and butter or a fruit spread. Scrambled egg can also be offered once or twice a week.

Lunch

I have always found it better to give my babies their daily serving of protein at lunchtime as opposed to teatime. Babies of this age can often get tired and irritable by 5pm and may be a bit fussier about eating. If they have had a well-balanced meal of protein and vegetables at lunchtime, you can be a bit more relaxed about what they have at teatime.

If, for some reason, your baby doesn't have his daily serving of protein at lunchtime, include some grated cheese for tea. Vegetables should be lightly steamed and chopped. Try to ensure that you vary the selection from day to day so that your baby is aware of the different colours and textures.

It is also important not to overload your baby's plate at this stage – an overfull plate can put some babies off, and with others it can lead to a game of throwing food on the floor. Serve up a small amount and, if he finishes it, offer more. If he does start to play up at mealtimes, refusing to eat or throwing his food on the floor, remove his plate immediately. It is very important not to get into a habit of force feeding or cajoling your baby to eat.

Babies of this age very quickly learn to fuss and refuse their main course if they know they will be offered a treat such as fromage frais or a biscuit. If your baby doesn't eat well at lunchtime, offer him a piece of fruit or cheese mid-afternoon, to see him through to teatime.

A very hungry baby may need a serving of fruit and yoghurt in addition to his savoury lunch. A drink of well-diluted, pure, unsweetened orange or apple juice will help the absorption of iron at this meal. However, it is very important to try to get your baby to have most of his solids before offering him a drink. Allowing him to drink too much before his meal may considerably reduce his appetite.

By the end of the first year your baby should be able to eat much the same as the rest of the family and it is important that some of his meals are integrated with yours – this is how he will learn table manners.

When preparing family meals, cook without salt, sugar and unnecessary additives, reserve your baby's portion, then add the desired flavourings for the rest of the family.

Tea

During the weaning stage your baby should be offered a wide variety of finger foods, and these are ideal for teatime. Savoury sandwiches, small pieces of pizza and chopped-up low-salt vegetarian sausages are good examples of finger food that can be given – served, say, with a thick soup, vegetable lasagne or vegetable bake.

Many babies will cut back or refuse their 2.30pm feed altogether at this stage. If you find that your baby's milk intake has dropped below 540ml (18oz), introduce foods such as cheesy vegetable bakes, mini quiches, baked potatoes with grated cheese, or vegetables and pasta in a milk sauce at teatime. Yoghurt and milk puddings can also be offered at teatime if you are concerned about your baby's milk intake.

By one year of age your baby's minimum daily milk intake requirement will drop to 350ml (12oz) and the bedtime bottle should be replaced by a drink from a beaker. To get him used to less milk at this last feed offer him a small amount from a beaker with his tea, followed by a drink of 150–180ml (5–6oz) from a beaker at bedtime.

Daily amounts needed at 9–12 months:

* Three to four servings of carbohydrate, made up of cereal, wholemeal bread, pasta or potatoes. One tablespoon of cereal or half a small baked potato is the equivalent of one serving.

* Three to four servings of fruit and vegetables, including raw vegetables. A serving is one small apple, pear, banana or carrot, a couple of cauliflower or broccoli florets or two tablespoons of chopped green beans.

* A serving of animal protein or two of vegetable protein. A serving is one tablespoon of poultry, meat or fish, or three tablespoons of pulses (lentils, peas, beans).

Third stage tips

* The amount of teeth your baby has and how well he can chew will be a guide as to when to introduce tougher foods, such as beef and harder fruits.

* Continue to avoid giving meats such as ham, bacon and sausages which are high in salt.

* Babies are very aware of colour and texture at this age, so try to make food look appealing and interesting. Avoid mashing and mixing his different foods together, and make

up a two-week menu plan to avoid giving the same foods too close together.

* Some babies may also need a snack mid-morning or mid-afternoon – try to offer healthy foods such as crackers, cheese and fruit. Avoid sweet and salty snacks, such as biscuits, cakes and crisps.

* It is important that large volumes of milk are discouraged by this stage. No more than 600ml (20oz), inclusive of milk used in food, should be allowed.

* Cow's milk can be introduced as a drink from the age of one year – it should be full fat, pasteurised and preferably organic.

Giving up formula

Some parents are keen to change from formula to milk earlier because they are finishing off a container of formula powder and are reluctant to buy more. However, I would suggest that they do buy the extra and either continue with the formula for an extra few weeks beyond their baby's first birthday or give the extra formula to a friend.

While I think it would probably be perfectly safe to switch the formula and use cow's milk when your baby is around 11 months, I would still advise you to wait until your child turns one to do so. That may sound confusing, so let me explain: guidelines like this and many others, from recommended vitamin intakes to not giving honey until the first birthday, are designed to take in the needs of just about all people. They take into account that people's bodies vary, and that some will develop and start to eat a balanced diet later than others. While most babies will decrease their need for the extra vitamins and other nutrients provided by formula before the age of one, a few may still need them if they have a lower intake of solid foods or higher body requirements. No harm will be done by waiting a little longer.

If you want to make a gradual transition, I'd suggest you just wait and start the process after your baby's birthday. There's no need to change all at once – many babies will protest at this. You can either change one drink at a time and see how your baby reacts, or make a mix of formula and milk, gradually decreasing the amount of formula so he ends up just drinking milk.

Case study: Theo, aged 11 months
Problem: Fussy feeding
Cause: Timing of drinks between meals and still using a bottle for milk

Theo had always been a good eater, enjoying a wide range of freshly cooked foods. At around eight months his mother noticed he was starting to reject more and more of his favourite meals. By the time she contacted me Theo had reached 10 months and mealtimes had become a complete battleground, with him clamping his mouth shut the minute a spoon was put anywhere near it. His mother would try lots of different tactics to try to get him back to his old eating habits. She would spend ages singing, clapping and playing all sorts of games at mealtimes to try to get Theo to smile so he would take just one extra mouthful. If this approach failed she would then try offering him endless choices of meals, with him often taking no more than a mouthful from each choice.

When I received Theo's food diary I could see that there were several very obvious things that were not helping his feeding problems. One was the timing of his drinks, which were too close to mealtimes and taking the edge off his appetite; another was the fact that Theo was still drinking his morning and evening milk from a bottle. He was consuming over 240ml (8oz) at both of these feeds, which was also taking the edge off his appetite.

I advised Theo's mother to offer him no more than 180ml (6oz) from a beaker first thing in the morning and no more than 210ml (7oz) from his bottle in the evening. These amounts, along with milk used in cereals, would still exceed 350ml (12oz), the minimum recommended at one year of age. Any other fluid should be offered midway between meals, not an hour before. At mealtimes I advised that Theo should not be given his juice until he had eaten at least half of his solids.

It was also obvious from the food diary that most of Theo's food was still being mashed and mixed up and that very little finger food was being offered. I explained that babies of Theo's age become interested in the colour, texture and shape of their food and I suspected he had become very bored with all his food still being mashed and mixed up into one bowl. It was very important to offer him a selection of finger foods at most meals and allow him to feed himself, regardless of how messy he got. Although I advise offering a selection of finger foods, the choice should not be endless.

At this age the amount a baby eats at individual meals can become very erratic and it is best never to force the baby to feed. Allow a certain length of time, but if it becomes obvious that he is not interested then clear the food away. He should not be coaxed or cajoled into eating – all babies will eat well if they are hungry enough and not overtired. It is best to judge a baby's food intake over several days at this age, not by what he eats at individual meals.

Theo's feeding did improve considerably, although he still had days when he was fussy. As he had just started learning to walk, I suspected that tiredness might also be a cause of his fussiness and I advised his mother to start his meals slightly earlier on days when he had been extremely energetic.

5
Feeding Problems

It is normal to hit some obstacles when you are weaning your baby. This chapter gives advice on how to easily overcome the most common problems.

Refusing solids

✿ Babies aged six months or older often refuse solids because they drink too much milk, especially if they are still feeding in the middle of the night. Milk is still the most important food for babies under six months, but the introduction of solids can be affected if feeds aren't structured.

* If your baby is six months old, taking five milk feeds a day and refusing solids, I would suggest you ask your health visitor about gradually reducing one of the milk feeds to encourage his interest in solids. If he has to be woken at 7am, I would advise cutting back gradually on the 10pm feed; if he is waking earlier than 7am, I suggest that you cut back on the 11am feed instead to encourage him to take solids then. Once he is happy taking solids at 11am, introduce some at the 6pm feed. As his appetite increases so will the amount of solids he takes, which will have the knock-on effect of him drinking less at the 10pm feed.

* By the end of six months a baby's milk intake should be around 600ml (20oz) a day, divided between three drinks a day and small amounts used in food. If your baby still refuses solids at this age, despite cutting down on his milk intake, it is important that you discuss the problem with your GP or health visitor.

Refusing milk

❀ The amount of milk a six-month-old baby drinks will gradually begin to reduce as his intake of solid food increases. However, up to the age of nine months a baby still needs a minimum of 540–600ml (18–20oz) a day of breast or formula milk. This daily amount gradually reduces to a minimum of 350ml (12oz) at one year of age. If your baby is losing interest or refusing some of his milk feeds and taking less than the recommended amounts, careful attention should be given to the timings of solids and the type of food given.

❀ Up to the age of six months a baby should still be taking a full feed morning and evening. A full feed consists of 210–240ml (7–8oz) or a feed from both breasts. Babies under six months who are given solids in the middle of their milk feed will be more likely to refuse the remainder of their formula or the second breast.

❀ A baby under five months of age still needs a full milk feed at 11am, even if he is being weaned early. Introducing breakfast too soon, or offering too much solid food first thing in the morning, can cause a baby to cut down too quickly or refuse the 11am feed.

* The 11am feed should be reduced gradually between the ages of five and six months (if weaning early under medical advice). Introducing the tier system of feeding (milk, solids, milk) before five months can also be the reason a baby refuses his milk at this feed.

* Giving lunchtime solids at 2pm and evening solids at 5pm is the reason many babies under six months cut down too quickly or refuse their 6pm feed. Until he reaches six months, it is better to give a baby his lunchtime solids at 11am and his evening solids after he has had a full milk feed at 6pm.

* Giving hard-to-digest foods, such as banana or avocado, at the wrong time of day can cause a baby to cut back on the next milk feed. Until a baby reaches six months, it is better to serve these types of food after the 6pm feed rather than during the day.

- Babies over six months of age who begin to refuse milk are often being allowed too many snacks in between meals or too much juice. Try replacing juice with water and cutting out snacks in between meals.

- Between 9 and 12 months some babies begin refusing the bedtime milk feed, which is a sign that they are ready to drop their third milk feed. If this happens, it is important to reduce the amount given at the afternoon feed before eventually dropping it altogether.

Case study: Josh, aged six months
Problem: Josh began to refuse his milk at about six months old
Cause: Introducing certain foods too early

Josh had been an easy and contented baby for his first five months. He was taking four full formula feeds a day, and sleeping well from 7pm to around 6.30am every night.

At five months Josh's mother, Clare, was advised to begin weaning. Clare initially introduced small amounts of first-stage weaning foods, plus some other fruits. But within a couple of weeks Josh's routine began to go awry. One night he woke, unusually, at 2am. Clare tried to settle him with a cuddle and some cooled boiled water but he could not be consoled, and continued to cry. This behaviour was so unlike Josh that Clare was concerned that he might be genuinely hungry as he had only taken 150ml (5oz) at the 6pm feed, so she decided to offer him a small 120ml (4oz) feed. Josh drank this quickly but still refused to settle back to sleep until he was given a further 120ml (4oz) of formula. He then settled back to sleep very quickly and had to be woken at 7am.

During the course of the following week Josh became more and more difficult over his daytime milk feeds, and a pattern soon emerged of his taking only 120–150ml (4–5oz) at each daytime feed, and only 90–120ml (3–4oz) at 6.15pm, before waking up desperately hungry between 2 and 3am.

At this point Clare called me, and we went through Josh's routines and feeding patterns up until this point. Clare had followed the Contented Little Baby routines for Josh's first months, and until the point when he began to wake at night the structure and timing of milk feeds and solids were correct.

However, I noticed that she had decided to introduce certain fibrous foods earlier than I recommend. I advise introducing banana at no earlier than six months, but, on the advice of a friend, Clare had added banana to Josh's breakfast cereal at five months. Josh loved banana, and this prompted his mother to offer it to him regularly at lunchtime along with mashed avocado, another food which I believe is difficult for babies to digest.

Clare had introduced meat at six months, and this had resulted in Josh cutting back too quickly on his milk intake. From my experience of weaning babies, I was able to establish that Clare had introduced too many food types that take longer to digest, too quickly, and as a consequence Josh had to wake in the night to make up for the milk he still needed – milk that he was no longer getting during the day. It was clear from the feeding charts that Josh, who then weighed 6.6kg (15lb), had cut back too dramatically on his milk intake during the day because his solids had been increased too rapidly (especially at breakfast). Clare, keen to increase the amount of milk he was taking, decided to mix more formula into his breakfast cereal, which resulted in his having eight teaspoonfuls of breakfast cereal plus mashed banana at breakfast.

I advised Clare to cut back the breakfast cereal to four teaspoonfuls, with one or two cubes of pear or peach purée instead of banana. Lunch generally consisted of six tablespoonfuls of a savoury casserole followed by rice and fruit, and was also contributing to Josh's decreasing appetite for milk. I suggested that Clare replace the rice and fruit with fruit and yoghurt. At teatime Josh was given another savoury dish, again usually made up of fish or chicken, mixed with rice and formula milk to help boost his milk intake. I advised Clare to replace the meat dish with some carbohydrates such as pasta or a baked potato with vegetables.

Within a week Josh had increased his three daytime milk feeds to 210–240ml (7–8oz) a feed. Although he *continued to wake up during the night for a further 10 days, I convinced his mother that it was now being caused by habit rather than a genuine need for milk, and she followed my suggestion of settling him back to sleep with some cooled boiled water. At the end of two weeks Josh was eating three well-balanced meals a day and drinking 690ml (23oz) of formula from the bottle and taking a further 120ml (4oz) of formula in his cereal.*

I believe that the types of food Josh was first weaned on were the cause of his rapid decrease of milk. Being given too much banana and avocado, and mixing sweet potato with baby rice, during the early stages of weaning causes babies under six months to cut back too quickly on their daytime milk. In Josh's case the problem was made even worse by the fact that he weighed only 6.6kg (15lb) and that he was being given meat twice a day as well as hard-to-digest foods.

It is a common mistake to introduce too much of the incorrect types of food too early or at the wrong time and thus create a problem of milk underfeeding. It is the main reason for babies under six months cutting back too quickly on their daytime milk, which results in a genuine need to feed in the night.

Fussy feeding

Preventing your child from becoming a fussy eater starts early. Children who are weaned appropriately on a varied diet are less likely to become fussy, but there are always exceptions to the rule. Even those who were weaned by the book can suddenly become fussy. Whatever the situation, don't use food as a reward or punishment, and never lose sight of the fact that children usually grow out of fussy eating and that it is not likely to have any long-term consequences. Far more damaging for your child is to have a constantly fretful and anxious parent.

If milk feeding is structured properly during the early days of weaning, the majority of babies will happily eat most of the foods they are offered. By the time they reach nine months babies should be getting most of their nourishment from eating three solid meals a day. Parents are advised to offer their babies a wide variety of foods to ensure they receive all the nutrients they need. However, it is often around this time that many babies start to reject food they have previously enjoyed. If your baby is between 9 and 12 months of age and suddenly starts to reject his food, or becomes fussy and fretful at mealtimes, the following guidelines should help determine the cause.

* Parents can have unrealistic expectations of the amounts of food their baby can eat, and serving over-large portions can mislead them into thinking their baby has a feeding problem. See recommended quantities on pages 86–7.

* Self-feeding plays an important role in a baby's mental and physical development as it encourages hand-to-eye co-ordination and increases his sense of independence. Between six and nine months of age most babies will start to pick up their food and try to feed themselves. This can be very messy and make mealtimes take much longer, but restricting a baby's natural desire to explore his food and feed himself will only lead to frustration and very often a refusal to be spoon-fed. Introducing lots of finger foods and allowing your baby to eat part of his meal by himself, regardless of the mess he makes, will make him much more inclined to take the remainder from you off a spoon.

* By the time a baby reaches nine months of age he will become more interested in the colour, shape and texture of his food. A baby who is still having all the different foods mashed up together will quickly begin to get bored with even his favourite foods, and this is one of the main reasons that babies lose interest in vegetables.

* Offering your baby a selection of vegetables of various textures and colours at each meal in small amounts will be more appealing to him than a large amount of just one or two vegetables.

* Sweet puddings and ice cream served on a regular basis are a major cause of babies refusing their main course. Even babies as young as nine months can quickly learn that if they refuse savoury foods and fuss enough they will more than likely be given the pudding. It is better to restrict puddings and desserts to special occasions, and serve your baby fresh fruit, yoghurt or cheese as a second course.

* If your baby rejects a particular food it is important to offer it again a couple of weeks later. Babies' likes and dislikes regarding food fluctuate a good deal in the first year, and parents who don't persist with trying rejected foods often find that their baby ends up eating a very restricted diet.

* Giving large amounts of juice or water before a meal can stop a baby feeding well. Try to offer him drinks midway

between meals, not an hour before. At mealtimes, encourage him to eat at least half of his solids before offering him a drink of water or well-diluted fresh juice.

✿ The timing of meals also plays a big part in how well a baby eats. A baby who is having his breakfast solids later than 8am is unlikely to be very hungry before 1pm. Likewise, a baby who is having teatime solids later than 5pm may be too tired to eat well.

✿ Hard-to-digest snacks, such as bananas or cheese, can often take the edge off a baby's appetite. Try restricting snacks for a couple of days to see if your baby's appetite improves at mealtimes.

✿ If you are concerned that your baby is not taking enough solids, seek advice from your health visitor or GP. Keep a diary for a week listing the times and amounts of all food and drink consumed, as this will help you determine the cause of your baby's feeding problems.

Introducing a beaker

Making the transition to taking milk from a beaker rather than a bottle is another stepping stone towards your baby's growing independence. Not allowing them to exercise this desire and develop their independence can, in many cases, lead to milk/food refusal. If you do not introduce the beaker, before you know it you may have a toddler who's having large bottle feeds several times a day and stubbornly refusing to drink out of a beaker, or even refusing milk altogether once the bottles are taken away. As with weaning your baby on to solid foods, when making the move from bottle to beaker, persevere and be consistent – your baby will soon adapt. Aim to have phased out bottles altogether by the time your baby is a year old.

✿ Once your baby reaches six to seven months of age and is established on a proper protein meal at lunchtime he no longer needs milk at that feed, and this would be a good time to introduce a beaker.

* He should be offered cool boiled water or well-diluted juice halfway through the meal and after every few mouthfuls. Many babies take quite a while to get used to drinking from a beaker and will only drink a very small amount in the first few weeks of its introduction. It is important to persevere. Experiment with different types of beaker until you find one that seems to suit your baby.

* If your baby is taking only a very small amount of fluid from a beaker at 11.45am, he may need to be offered extra milk at the 2pm feed or extra cool boiled water later in the day.

* Once he is accustomed to drinking water or well-diluted juice from a beaker, milk can be introduced in a beaker at either the 7am feed or the 2pm feed. This should ideally happen somewhere between the eighth and ninth month, preparing your baby for taking all his drinks from a beaker by one year.

* Experts recommend that all bottle-feeding is stopped by the age of one year, as it can remove the appetite for other

foods. In my experience, babies who continue milk-feeding from a bottle past the age of one year will often refuse milk altogether when the bottle is eventually stopped.

Case study: Flora, aged five and a half months
Problem: Flora was initially enthusiastic regarding weaning but quickly went off anything other than fruit purées
Cause: A sweet tooth, which was unintentionally encouraged

Louisa approached me when Flora was five and a half months old. Flora had settled easily into the Contented Little Baby method, and was a happy little baby. By the time Flora was five months old, she was a healthy weight and was drinking up to 330ml (11oz) of formula at each feed. After a discussion with her health visitor, Louisa decided to begin weaning Flora.

At first Flora was reluctant to take solids, but Louisa persisted slowly. Once Flora was established on baby rice, Louisa introduced her to pear. Flora loved this fruit, and with this as an encouragement Louisa tried her on vegetables. Apparently this did not go well – Louisa tried carrot, sweet potato and butternut squash, but Flora refused everything apart from a variety of fruit purées. Within three weeks of being introduced to solids, Flora was very upset to be offered anything other than fruit purées, and would respond by arching her back in her high chair and refusing to open her mouth.

It was at this point Louisa contacted me. I thought that it was likely that Flora had a sweet tooth, and that the pattern of weaning that Louisa described had unintentionally encouraged this. Louisa accepted that we would need to address this, and I reassured her that with the right encouragement it would be something that we could resolve.

We immediately began by taking Flora back to stage one of the weaning process, offering her small amounts of vegetable purées with baby rice, and for the time being eliminating the fruit purées. The next couple of weeks proceeded with varying degrees of success. On one or two days Flora was prepared to eat vegetable purées but most of the time she was upset to be offered this rather than her preferred fruit purées, and would refuse to try the vegetables and rice. It was difficult for Louisa but she persevered, and after a couple of weeks Flora accepted a spoonful of carrot and green bean purée on its own. Louisa was thrilled, and felt that this approach was the right one. Once this lunchtime routine was firmly established, and Flora was happily eating her vegetables and baby rice, I advised Louisa that it was time to reintroduce a small mouthful of fruit purée at the end of the meal. Flora loved this!

Teatime meals were much easier – Flora was always enthusiastic about her fruit and rice. By six months she was happily eating a good meal of rice and fruit at teatime.

At this point Flora was back on track, and I didn't speak to Louisa again for a few weeks. During this time, when Flora was about six and a half months old, Louisa decided to introduce protein. This change initially ran smoothly. Once Flora was happily eating eight cubes of protein and vegetables, Louisa thought it would be nice to replace a couple of those cubes with fruit purée as dessert at lunchtime. Flora's teatime meal comprised of a couple of cubes of protein with six teaspoons of rice, and this was followed by a couple more cubes of fruit purée with four more teaspoons of rice. In addition, Louisa started to feed Flora a small amount of cereal at breakfast time.

Just before Flora turned seven months old she began to get very upset during lunchtime again. When Louisa offered her a spoonful of food she began to cry, she arched her back and clamped her mouth tightly shut. If Louisa reverted to baby rice, she managed to persuade Flora to eat some savoury food, but otherwise mealtimes became upsetting again. Louisa wondered if Flora's appetite had decreased, so she attempted to reduce the number of cubes offered. This did not seem to help things, and it was only the fruit offered at the end of the meal that Flora was prepared to eat enthusiastically. Once again, Louisa had been inadvertently encouraging Flora's sweet tooth. She tried *every distraction to persuade Flora to try the savoury meals – singing, encouraging chat, smiles, warming the food, cooling it, making it a more sauce-like consistency, adding more rice, altering the times and so on. There might have been a slight improvement for a couple of days but then Flora would become really cross again and refuse to eat anything.*

When we next spoke, it was clear to me that Flora was resisting solids at every meal. I advised that for the next week we concentrate on establishing two good meals a day. To do this we needed to temporarily cut out breakfast and bring forward lunch. So two days before Flora turned seven months we introduced a new feeding plan. Louisa gave Flora 195ml (6½oz) formula to drink at breakfast. Lunch was brought forward to 10.30am and Louisa just served protein and vegetables. If Flora still appeared to be hungry after six cubes of savoury food, then Louisa gave her a couple of teaspoons of rice mixed with formula. She then had 210ml (7oz) of formula after her lunchtime nap.

I advised cutting out protein at teatime and replacing this with a high-carbohydrate tea. Louisa had explained that since she had introduced protein at her teatime meal Flora had been waking up much earlier – between 5.45 and 6am, with a full nappy. Prior to this Flora had always been a good sleeper, waking at 7am.

For the short term Louisa avoided giving Flora fruit at all. Within a week Flora was eating six cubes of protein and vegetables at lunchtime, and this was sometimes followed by a couple of teaspoons of rice. At teatime, around 5pm, Louisa offered her three cubes of vegetables combined with six teaspoons of rice and formula. This was followed by another 4–5 teaspoons of rice and formula. At bedtime Flora drank 240–270ml (8–9oz) formula.

Flora continues to eat a nourishing, well-balanced meal plan. Her tricky behaviour has become a thing of the past, and mealtimes are no longer the battle that they had become, which distressed both Louisa and Flora.

Constipation

With any case of constipation it's always a good idea to look at fluid intake first, as the best diet in the world for babies or adults won't help if fluid intake is too low. As your baby is weaning and increasing his intake of solids, he may naturally be cutting down his fluid intake at this time. You could try offering extra breast-feeds if he is breast-fed, or drinks of water to complement his formula. You could also try offering some of his drinks before meals if his fluid intake seems low.

Papaya has a reputation for relieving constipation, but there doesn't seem to be any scientific evidence for it being any more effective than other fruits. It is safe to give as an early weaning food. As with other fruits and vegetables, the fibre it contains will help to some extent.

Prunes, on the other hand, are known to contain a chemical other than the fibre that promotes bowel movement. They contain sorbitol, a form of sugar that is used in some diet foods such as diet chewing gum and diet sweets. You may recall that packets of these foods can carry the warning that consumption of excessive amounts may have a laxative effect. This is because the sorbitol is digested very slowly in the body and holds extra water in the bowel, making a softer and larger stool that is easier to pass. In addition, researchers long ago discovered that prunes contained a substance very similar to some laxative medications, though recent studies have not been able to repeat this result. However, this may be another reason why prunes are renowned for helping with constipation, so we must take extra care when introducing them to children's diets.

I'd suggest trying to increase fluid first if intake seems low, then adding just half a teaspoon of puréed prune at a time, first at one then two meals a day. Then increase it by an extra half teaspoon a day until you notice an effect (up to a tablespoon or two a day at this age).

Pears also have a reputation for relieving constipation. They contain a type of fibre that is different to other fruit and vegetables, which helps add extra bulk to stools, making them easier to pass. Thus they may be more effective than other choices.

As your child progresses with weaning, you'll be able to offer her fruit and vegetables chopped as finger foods rather than as a purée. This can help with constipation as the foods are less processed so the fibre remains more intact, and more effective at moving bowels along. Puréed fruit is better than juice, but mashed fruit is better, and chopped fruit more effective again. Of course, as your child gets older you can start introducing some wholegrain, unrefined foods (wheat and rice fibre are among the most effective types), but this is too much bulk for a little baby.

If you find the fluid, prunes and other fruit and vegetables are not helping then you should seek advice from your health visitor or GP.

Conclusion

Babies learn by example so once your baby has been introduced to a wide variety of different foods, and established on three meals a day, it is important to include him in as many family meals as possible. If work commitments make this difficult at least try to eat together at breakfast time, plus lunchtime at the weekends. Family mealtimes give you the ideal opportunity to teach your baby how to feed himself, use cutlery properly and establish healthy eating habits and good social skills where food is concerned.

Including your baby in family meals is particularly important if you have a toddler or older children, as preparing two or even three different meals a day is not only time-consuming but can take the pleasure out of family meals. It will also enable you to offer your baby a wide variety of different foods at each meal, without getting stressed if he refuses some of them. One important thing to note when you are cooking for the whole family is to remember not to use salt or pepper. When serving the meal remove the children's portions, then add seasoning to the rest.

As your baby nears the end of his first year, it is important to realise that he is becoming more independent and will develop likes and dislikes to certain foods. It is important not to get into a battle of wills with him regarding food. Offer him a variety and try not to force him to eat certain foods if he refuses them. Leave them out of his diet for a couple of weeks and then reintroduce them. More likely than not, he will accept the food he so stubbornly refused previously.

For ideas on creating meals that the whole family can enjoy, you can refer to *The Gina Ford Baby and Toddler Cook Book* and *Feeding Made Easy*. These books include recipes and menu planners that are suited to the needs of a family trying to feed children of different ages as well as their parents. There are quick and easy recipes for a weekday supper, weekday lunches after nursery and/or preschool, and family meals at the weekend, as well as ideas for baking, puddings and birthday party food. All the recipes can be adapted for the whole family.

Wishing you very many happy mealtimes with your contented baby.

Useful Resources

Allergy UK
Helpline: 01322 619898
www.allergyuk.org

CASH (Concensus Action on Salt and Health)
Tel: 020 7882 5941
www.actiononsalt.org.uk

Food Standards Agency
Tel: 020 7276 8829
www.food.gov.uk

The Foundation for the Study of Infant Deaths (FSID)
Helpline: 0808 802 6868
www.fsid.org.uk

The Great Little Trading Company
Tel: 0844 848 6000
www.gltc.co.uk

La Leche League
Tel: 0845 456 1855
www.laleche.org.uk

NCT (The National Childbirth Trust)
Tel: 0300 330 0770
www.nct.org.uk

So Baby Limited
Tel: 01829 772 555
www.so-baby.co.uk

Soil Association
Tel: 0117 314 5000
www.soilassociation.org

Sure Start
Tel: 08002 346 346
www.direct.gov.uk/surestart

Twins and Multiple Births Association (TAMBA)
Tel: 01483 304442
Twinline: 0800 138 0509
www.tamba.org.uk

Vegetarian Society
Includes advice on a gluten-free diet
Tel: 0161 925 2000
www.vegsoc.org

Visit Gina Ford's website: www.contentedbaby.com

Further Reading

Potty Training in One Week by Gina Ford (Vermilion, 2003)

The Gina Ford Baby and Toddler Cook Book by Gina Ford (Vermilion, 2005)

The Contented Child's Food Bible by Gina Ford (Vermilion, 2005)

The New Contented Little Baby Book by Gina Ford (Vermilion, 2006)

The Contented Toddler Years by Gina Ford (Vermilion, 2006)

The Contented Little Baby Book of Weaning by Gina Ford (Vermilion, 2006)

The Complete Sleep Guide for Contented Babies and Toddlers by Gina Ford (Vermilion, 2006)

A Contented House with Twins by Gina Ford and Alice Beer (Vermilion, 2006)

Gina Ford's Top Tips for Contented Babies and Toddlers by Gina Ford (Vermilion, 2006)

The Contented Baby's First Year by Gina Ford (Vermilion, 2007)

Feeding Made Easy by Gina Ford (Vermilion, 2008)

The Contented Baby with Toddler Book by Gina Ford (Vermilion, 2009)

From Crying Baby to Contented Baby by Gina Ford (Vermilion, 2010)

Top Tips for Fussy Eaters by Gina Ford (Vermilion, 2010)

Contented Baby Newsletter

To learn more about the Contented Baby routines and Gina Ford's books visit Gina's official websites at www.contentedbaby.com and www.contentedtoddler.com and sign up to receive Gina's free monthly newsletter, which is full of useful information, tips and advice as well as answers to questions about parenting issues and even a recipe or two.

You may also want to take the opportunity to become part of Gina's online community by joining one or both of the websites. As a member you'll receive a monthly online magazine with a personal message from Gina, along with a selection of the latest exclusive features on topical issues from our guest contributors and members. You'll be able to access more than 2,000 frequently asked questions about feeding, sleeping and development answered by Gina and her team, as well as many case histories not featured in the Contented Little Baby series of books.

www.contentedbaby.com

www.contentedtoddler.com

www.contentedbaby.com/shop-directory.htm

Contented Baby Consultation Service

Gina offers a one-to-one personal telephone consultation service for parents who wish for specialist help in establishing healthy feeding and sleeping habits, as laid out in the Contented Baby and Toddler routine books. If you would like further details of how a personal consultation with Gina works, we would request that in the first instance you send a detailed feeding and sleeping diary for 48 hours, along with a concise summary of what you think your problem is, using the contact form on www.contentedbaby.com.

Gina Ford and So Baby
Superior Ready-made Meals

Gina has spent several months working with organic baby-food supplier So Baby, developing a range of pure, organic baby meals. Unlike other baby-food suppliers, So Baby never use fillers, additives or anything unnatural in order to bulk up meals, just pure, locally sourced organic ingredients. Each and every meal is prepared by hand in their organic kitchen, cooked naturally, then frozen – just as you'd do at home. No other large-scale baby-food producer does this. For further information, see www.contentedbaby.com or www.so-baby.co.uk.